CHANEL

STYLE ICON

CHANEL

STYLE ICON

A CELEBRATION OF THE TIMELESS
STYLE OF COCO CHANEL

MAGGIE DAVIS

Hardie Grant

BOOKS

Contents

Introduction

Few fashion designers command such awe and respect as Gabrielle 'Coco' Chanel. As style icons go, she is at the very top of the league. Her meteoric rise from the depths of hardship to the heady heights of fashion superstardom is the stuff of fairy tales. Chanel is responsible for radically changing the way women dressed and, perhaps more importantly, felt about dressing in the 20th century. She lived by the maxim, 'A dress that isn't comfortable is a dress that has failed.' One of her main goals as a designer? 'Enabling women to move with ease, to not feel like they are in costume,' as she once put it. A simple yet completely liberating concept.

A poor French girl with a shock of black hair and a mind full of ideas, Chanel began her story in a small town in the Loire Valley. One of five children, she was destined to spend several years between a strict Catholic orphanage and her aunt's house after her mother died suddenly of tuberculosis. From lowly beginnings, the seeds for Chanel's future were sown when she showed a passion for needlework. Combined with her striking beauty and steely determination, it would help pave her way out of poverty and into the higher echelons of Parisian society. She would capture the hearts of many male admirers, from Arthur 'Boy' Capel to the Duke of Westminster, who were all instrumental in helping Chanel establish a fashion empire.

Through a combination of ambition, clear vision and a natural charm that could entrance anyone she set her sights on, Chanel achieved phenomenal success. She became close friends with aristocrats, politicians, artists and writers, all of them drawn to her radiance. Chanel surrounded herself with those who would enrich and inspire her. And yet, her natural allure, wit and warmth meant her relationships were reciprocal; she was hugely respected and revered in her circles. Through her connections, she was able to realise her vision and launch her label in Paris, Deauville and Biarritz before becoming a global phenomenon.

Throughout her life, Chanel created many defining style moments: from her early days establishing her label in the 1910s, through her time as a world-renowned designer in the 1920s to her monumental comeback in the 1950s. Crucially, Chanel remained the ultimate model for her designs from her days as a milliner in Paris, where she wore – with easy elegance – the hats she was selling, to the cool jersey cardigans she rocked in the 1920s. Then there were the glamorous evening dresses of the 1930s, layered with multiple strands of pearls, and the chic tweed suits of the 1960s. Nobody defined Chanel better than Coco.

As you'll see in the pages that follow, the designer herself was the ultimate style icon. All her major looks and achievements, from the Little Black Dress (LBD) to the tweed suit, were inspired by her own desire for simple, elegant and easy-to-wear attire. Yet, along the way, Chanel also enlisted a host of glamorous wearers – women who, at a given moment, defined the label. From actresses Ina Claire in the 1930s and Romy Schneider in the 1950s to Jackie Kennedy in the 1960s, there were many key Chanel women. It was a tradition that Karl Lagerfeld maintained when he took over as creative director of Chanel in 1983, serving up Chanel to a bold new generation of stylish and influential women.

Lagerfeld, known for his exceptional intelligence and creative flair, delved into the Chanel archive, but knew he had to push the label to new frontiers in order for it to survive. He did this by playing with and enhancing all the iconic Chanel pieces, from the quilted bag to the tweed suit, with wit, verve and, on occasion, huge controversy. With the help of models including Ines de la Fressange, Claudia Schiffer and Stella Tennant, Lagerfeld delivered Chanel to the modern woman. He pushed boundaries and yet always stayed respectful to Gabrielle Chanel's vision – just as his long-term, right-hand woman and successor as Chanel creative director, Virginie Viard, has done. The spirit of Chanel lives on.

1

In the Beginning

A humble start

Coco Chanel. Few names conjure luxury in quite the same way as hers does, but the designer's beginnings were far from glamorous. Born in the market town of Saumur, in the Loire Valley, central France, on 19 August 1883, Gabrielle Bonheur Chanel started life in the most modest circumstances possible – in the poorhouse. She was one of five children, and her mother Eugénie Jeanne Devolle (known as Jeanne), a washerwoman, and father Albert Chanel, a hapless peddler of no fixed abode, struggled to provide for their brood.

In 1895, Jeanne died of tuberculosis and Albert was unable to cope with the demands of looking after his children. The story goes that after sending his two sons, Alphonse and Lucien, to become farmhands, he packed his three daughters, Julia-Berthe, Gabrielle and Antoinette, off to an orphanage in a buggy cart.

While much of her childhood remains shrouded in myth and mystery, it's believed Chanel spent time in the medieval village of Aubazine, home to the 12th-century abbey founded by St Étienne. With its high walls, a steep pitched roof and a dark, austere interior – the kind that has inspired numerous horror movies – the orphanage provided a harsh backdrop for part of Chanel's childhood, and one that she frequently denied or embellished later in life.

The nuns were devout and strict – and it was they who introduced a young Chanel to needlework. Despite the hardship, Aubazine provided the foundations for Chanel's future career.

Life in the orphanage

Sleeping on a hard iron bedstead, eating gruel for breakfast, and enduring six days of strict Catholic schooling each week were a likely reality for the children at the orphanage. At times, so bleak was Chanel's childhood that she frequently thought that death would be a preferable option. 'I was thoroughly unhappy. I fed on sorrow and horror, I wanted to kill myself I don't know how many times,' she later told the writer Paul Morand, to whom she entrusted her memoirs.

During her childhood, Chanel and her sisters also spent time at the home of Anaïs Clouvel, her mother's first cousin, who ran a small laundry business and who she called an aunt. She talked to various biographers including Marcel Haedrich and Claude Delay about spending time with various aunts, and how cleanliness and needlework predominated. She sometimes denied being at Aubazine altogether, but the influence it had over her life and designs tells us otherwise.

Aubazine provided a strangely inspiring backdrop for Chanel – its austerity perhaps influenced her love of clean lines, the absence of fussiness, the monochromatic colour palette and symbols, such as the Maltese cross, that would become important elements throughout her career. Even the monochrome stained-glass windows of Aubazine are reminiscent of Chanel's instantly recognisable double-C logo, with looping circles that interlock in a spookily similar way. Everything, from the dark wooden furniture and whitewashed walls to the spartan staircase in the main hall – which she had replicated for her Côte d'Azur villa La Pausa – would end up inspiring Chanel throughout her life.

The young seamstress

Much of Chanel's education at Aubazine revolved around needlework, and it was there that she learned the practical skills that laid the foundations for her future career as the world's most celebrated couturier. Apparently, one of the tasks she undertook was hemming sheets – it was arduous and laborious, but something that required skill and meticulous attention to detail.

Chanel was dextrous and had a natural aptitude for sewing, but she yearned for something more: success, power and money. Even in the depths of hardship and with limited experience of the outside world, Chanel had the realisation that money would give her freedom: 'Without money, you are nothing, with money you can do anything … I would say to myself over and over, "Money is the key to freedom." She just had to work out a way of making it using her skills.

Coming of age

Throughout her teens, Chanel maintained contact with her paternal grandparents and became close to their youngest daughter, her aunt Adrienne, who was only a year older. According to Chanel's biographer Edmonde Charles-Roux, Adrienne was a pupil at the Notre Dame finishing school in the small town of Moulins, and so it was decided that Chanel would also attend, possibly as a non-paying 'charity' pupil.

Notre Dame school was run by canonesses who Chanel thought were a lot less fearsome than the nuns at Aubazine. Despite excelling at singing and the piano, she was treated as inferior by both the paying pupils and canonesses. But that didn't thwart the aspiring designer, who focused on enhancing her appearance. Looking back at pictures of her from this time, Karl Lagerfeld observed, 'Chanel was like a rural Audrey Hepburn.' Furthering their needlework skills, Chanel and Adrienne became experts at darning and also embellished their austere black uniforms by making cuffs and collars from white linen remnants. Clearly, there were already signs of what was to come.

'MY LIF

PLEA

SO I CI

MY I

DIDN'T

E ME,

EATED

FE.'

— COCO CHANEL

Dancing girl

Moulins, a picturesque town in the Auvergne-Rhône-Alpes region, became Chanel's launchpad. She and Adrienne found sewing work in a local tailoring shop and shared a room above it. While she worked as a seamstress by day, Chanel turned into a cabaret performer by night. 'I was becoming pretty. I had a face that was as plump as a fist, hidden by a vast swathe of black hair that reached the ground,' Chanel remembered later in life.

She danced and sang in a local club, La Rotonde, making money by passing around a hat after her performances. The patrons – many of them cavalry officers – were entranced by Chanel and she became one of the star performers. It was here that, according to fashion legend, Chanel earned the nickname Coco from two numbers she performed: 'Ko Ko Ri Ko' and 'Qui qu'a vu Coco dans l'Trocadéro?' Later, when trying to gloss over her troubled childhood, Chanel told biographer Claude Delay that her father had given her the endearing pet name. Either way, who could have known the nickname would become synonymous with one of the world's most luxurious brands.

Tomboy chic

In 1906, Chanel met Étienne Balsan, a French textiles heir and racehorse owner who took an instant shine to her. Within a year she had moved into his château in Royallieu, just outside Paris, as his lover (though Émilienne d'Alençon, an actress and courtesan, remained his 'official' mistress).

Although Chanel had to dine with the servants, she did have access to Balsan's horses. It was here that she became a fearless rider, refusing to ride side-saddle and therefore having to wear jodhpurs. She loathed the corseted, overly frivolous clothes fashionable at the time and revelled in a more boyish, sporty style that made her stand out. She took her style inspiration not from the aristocratic women she rubbed shoulders with but from jockeys, grooms and stable boys, and was already enthused by practical clothes that allowed free movement of the body but still looked elegant.

Chanel in love

Balsan had introduced Chanel to high society and she was grateful for that, and for the kindness and comfort he had provided, but she was never truly in love with him. It was on a trip with Balsan to Pau in southwestern France, in the romantic Pyrenees mountains, that she met Arthur 'Boy' Capel.

'In Pau, I met an Englishman ... when we were out horse-trekking one day; we all lived on horseback ... The young man was handsome, very tanned and attractive. More than handsome, he was magnificent. I admired his nonchalance, and his green eyes ... I fell in love with him,' Chanel told Paul Morand of her first encounter with Capel. Here she is pictured with Capel on the beach in Saint-Jean-de-Luz, around 1915

Capel was an English heir and playboy who shared Balsan's passion for horses and beautiful women. He was from a wealthy Catholic family and, with his English charm and fine looks, was irresistible to Chanel. The feeling was mutual: Capel was attracted to Chanel's beauty and enigmatic personality. By 1909, at the age of 26, Chanel had left Balsan at Royallieu and hopped on a train to Paris to be with Capel. Her adventure in fashion was about to begin.

2

A Fashion Star is Rising

COCO'S METEORIC ASCENT TO THE STYLE STRATOSPHERE

Hats on!

Chanel is known for many designs, from the quilted bag to the little black dress, but her first foray into serious design was as a milliner. She had already dabbled in hat styling at Royallieu, tweaking and trimming headpieces for actress Émilienne d'Alençon and other society women who loved her low-key, chic approach. Chanel would buy hats, such as simple straw boaters, at the upmarket Parisian department store Galeries Lafayette and add 'just a touch of something on top'. Later in life, she remembered of the races, 'In the grandstands, people began talking about my amazing, unusual hats.'

Encouraged by her lover, Boy Capel, Chanel was able to start a business in Paris. At first, she used former beau Étienne Balsan's bachelor pad on boulevard Malesherbes, but she was soon ready to open her first shop, funded by Capel. In 1910 she opened Chanel Modes at 21 rue Cambon, near the Ritz hotel, and it soon became an essential stop-off for the wealthy women staying there. Actresses began to wear her hats. 'I became something of a celebrity. I started a fashion ... Everybody wanted to meet me,' remembered Chanel.

Chanel remained her own ultimate model and appeared in a series of portraits wearing her own designs – large black fedoras adorned with a simple plume of feathers – and looking the epitome of chic. A designer-led brand had been born.

Sports chic

The overnight success of her hat shop gave Chanel the confidence to open her second shop just two years later. Her first fashion boutique, also funded by Capel, was in the fashionable Normandy seaside resort of Deauville, with its famous racecourse, casino and buzzing art scene. Chanel chose the town's most stylish street, rue Gontaut-Biron, for this new venture.

Deauville became popular as World War 1 loomed, and the affluent women who decamped there found themselves in need of fine clothes. Chanel observed them walking awkwardly around in restrictive corsets, heavy furs and cumbersome layers, and realised an overhaul was needed: sporty, comfortable clothing befitting of the seaside setting.

Inspired by the clothes of local sailors, the jockeys she had observed at the races and menswear in general – men seemed more comfortably attired at all times – Chanel started selling elegant turtleneck sweaters, sailor blouses and simple, sporty frocks made from jersey. She wanted women to be able to enjoy the beach, the sun and the outdoor life, and her designs were an instant hit, perfectly in sync with the modern woman's outlook.

Chanel was the epitome of seaside chic – the way she looked and the beachwear she designed encapsulated her sporty new look with easy elegance. No wonder France's most stylish women were in awe of her.

The queen of monochrome

Chanel's designs provided an antidote to the showy, bold colours made fashionable by designers such as Paul Poiret in the decadent 1900s. With World War I underway since 1914, frivolity seemed inappropriate, and Chanel had a knack of sensing the mood of the times. She knew that modern style ought not be ostentatious. 'Fashion should express the place, the moment,' Chanel famously said. A sober, monochrome colour palette felt just right.

Beige, black, and white – Chanel favoured plain shades that suited everyone. It was the austere colour palette of her childhood at Aubazine, evident in everything from the nun's habits to the clean lines of the Cistercian abbey and its paved mosaic floors.

In 1920, Chanel observed the audience at the opera with disdain – the women sported emerald greens, bold reds and royal blues. She recalled thinking, 'These colours are impossible. These women, I'm bloody well going to dress them in black.' Decades later, Chanel declared, 'I imposed black, it's still going strong today, for black wipes out everything else'.

Trousers for women!

By the 1920s, there were three trendsetting women wearing trousers: Hollywood stars Marlene Dietrich and Greta Garbo, and Coco Chanel. Chanel, a trouser trailblazer, had been inspired by both the formal attire and the sporting clothes of her high-society beaus. A keen rider and sportswoman herself, she relished the practicality and comfort of trousers and, to flatter her form, had slightly adapted the jodhpurs she had worn when she first met polo player and love of her life, Boy Capel. 'Nothing is more beautiful than freedom of the body,' Chanel famously declared.

Throughout her career, she experimented with different trouser cuts: high-waisted styles, neatly cinched at the waist and worn with a simple Breton top, lounge pyjamas that could be worn day or night, and elegant pantaloons.

Chanel always remained the best model for her styles – one of her most iconic trouser looks was on the beach in Venice in 1937. She wore white wide-legged trousers with a string of pearls, a black turtleneck, a black beret and an embellished cuff, setting the tone for decades to come.

Sailor style

We have many things for which to thank Gabrielle Chanel, and the suits-everyone Breton top is definitely one of them. Taking inspiration directly from the sailors she observed during her 1910s seaside jaunts to Northern France, Chanel saw that the garment was not only practical but that it had a nonchalant elegance, too.

The Breton was originally introduced in 1858 as the uniform for French seamen, featuring 21 stripes that represented each one of Napoleon Bonaparte's military victories. Stripes could be easily spotted in the sea, in cases of emergency, and the cut was comfortable but not so loose that it could get caught.

Chanel could see their appeal and introduced them to her nautical collection of 1917. Ta-dah! Chanel elevated the humble Breton to the height of fashion and it endured as a symbol of style and sophistication throughout the 20th century, adopted by artists from Pablo Picasso to Andy Warhol, and style icons including movie stars Audrey Hepburn and Marlon Brando. Later, French rebel designer Jean Paul Gaultier reinvented it with a punky new edge in the 1980s. But it was Chanel who wore it best – with a simple pair of flares, pumps and a nonchalant smile. Nobody did it better.

'I SIM
SOME
EVER
BECAUS
SOME
EVERY

PLIFY
THING
DAY
I LEARN
THING
DAY.'

— COCO CHANEL

Biarritz fix

In 1915, with Europe in the throes of World War I, Chanel had gone to Biarritz in the South of France with Boy Capel. As Spain had remained neutral in the war, its wealthy elite were still holidaying and indulging in luxury, and many affluent people from across France had also decamped there. Chanel spotted the opportunity and, with Boy's financial backing, opened her first fashion house, or *maison de couture*. The chic resort in the Bay of Biscay proved the perfect setting for her boutique, which employed a few hundred seamstresses.

Chanel immediately made a statement in her new boutique, with higher hemlines, relaxed silhouettes with no waistlines and, of course, jersey fabric – the humble material for which she became famous. This understated but stealthily luxurious style was perfectly in step with the times.

Chanel modelled her styles on the beach of Biarritz with a relaxed suit, white gloves and boyish two-tone brogues, the picture of elegance. Her legendary Biarritz collection, awash with jersey and relaxed silhouettes, was an instant hit, and Chanel was the new darling of the fashion world.

Masculine tailoring

Her days at Royallieu, with Étienne Balsan's stable of horses, had also proved significant in the evolution of Chanel's aesthetic. 'I cut jerseys from the sweaters the stable lads wore and from the knitted training garments I wore myself,' remembered Chanel in her old age.

Chanel biographer and a longtime editor of French *Vogue*, Edmonde Charles-Roux, visited Royallieu and met Balsan's old tailor Leroy and revealed how Chanel would experiment with her lover's clothes. She had taken one of Balsan's suits, and a shirt and tie, fashioning them into a new shape to fit her own slim physique. When Balsan saw that she had cut the sleeves off one of his favourite suits he was horrified, but Chanel had a way of doing exactly what she wanted.

Later, Chanel went to see the tailor with the modified suit and asked him to replicate it. Trousers, suits, shirts and later tweeds, usually the preserve of men, were all irresistible to Chanel, inspiring collections and her own style throughout her life. Once she translated that androgynous new style into designs for others, women the world over were soon delighted to cast off their corsets. A fashion revolution was underway.

The Parisian couture house is launched

Already a household name by 1918, Chanel was able to move to bigger premises at 31 rue Cambon, where her fashion house remains to this day. Crucially, she was now able to pay Boy Capel back in full, an important sign of her independence, and a timely one given his sudden death the following year. 'In a way, she bought her freedom,' Chanel's great-niece Gabrielle Palasse-Labrunie observed in *Intimate Chanel*. 'She was determined to pay Boy back and was proud of this money that she'd earned herself, through her hard work.'

At 31 rue Cambon, Chanel occupied the entire building – her modern boutique on the ground floor soon also stocked fragrance, accessories and jewellery alongside her fashion collections. With its large reception rooms, the first floor was used for fittings, and the iconic, much-photographed mirrored glass staircase led up to her second-floor apartment, which was filled with all her treasures – books, jewellery and antiques.

Chanel loved to recline on her chaise longue to read, always stylish, never compromising. Here, she is pictured wearing layered jewellery, a black hair bow and exuding an air of sophistication the rest of us can only dream of.

Riviera chic

Chanel saw being on the beach as an opportunity for women to show off their style, and it is no surprise that she yearned for a place by the ocean.

In 1928, she bought a plot of land overlooking the sparkling Mediterranean in Roquebrune-Cap-Martin on which to build a house. The villa she named La Pausa ('the pause') would become a place of refuge, but also the backdrop to her dazzling social life, boasting guests such as French poet and artist Jean Cocteau, Spanish artist Salvador Dalí, and her lover the Duke of Westminster. The Côte d'Azur had become a playground for a generation of fashionable creatives, and Chanel was about to become queen of them all.

Like her clothes, Chanel's sparse, airy villa was the height of chic. She enlisted architect Robert Streitz to visit her childhood orphanage at Aubazine and replicate the 12th-century staircase, with its imposing hallway, along with its arched windows and doors.

Designing La Pausa was a labour of love for Chanel, and she poured her heart into it. Bettina Wilson, from British *Vogue*, reported on one of her dinner parties in 1938: 'Mademoiselle Chanel, who eats very little anyway, is the prize entertainment, standing in front of a huge fireplace, making superb conversation, with gestures.' The whole setting and the way she dressed there – in silk pyjamas, tailored slacks and easy sailor shirts – defined the new Riviera chic.

The first power bob

'A woman who cuts her hair is about to change her life.' - Coco Chanel

In 1917, in a radical move, Chanel chopped her hair off. 'Because it annoyed me!' she said to Paul Morand in old age. 'And everyone went into raptures, saying that I looked like "a young boy, a little shepherd".' In another version, told to biographer Claude Delay, Chanel explained how she accidentally singed her hair with the gas boiler in her bathroom: 'My hair, which came down below my waist, was done up round my head in three braids – all that mass set straight upon that thin body ... There was a gas burner in the bathroom. I turned on the hot tap to wash my hands again, the water wasn't hot, so I fiddled with the pilot-light and the whole thing exploded. My white dress was covered in soot, my hair – the less said, the better.' She had no choice but to cut off her braids and went out to the opera with a head-turning blunt bob.

However Chanel's new hairstyle occurred, it set the tone for the 1920s. The bob became the hairstyle of the decade, worn by flappers and film stars including the iconic Louise Brooks, with women ditching over-styled locks in favour of this new, freer style.

Remarkably, the bob has remained in fashion pretty much ever since, and is still favoured by long-time editor-in-chief at American *Vogue* Anna Wintour. Perhaps one of the most significant things for which we have to say *merci beaucoup* to Chanel is this simple, no fuss, elegant and truly liberating hairstyle.

3

The Modern Designer

Mad about Misia

While Chanel had many lovers over her lifetime, she had only one true, enduring friend: pianist, muse and patron of the arts, Misia Sert. She was born Maria Zofia Olga Zenajda Godebska, in St Petersburg, and, like Chanel, suffered a difficult childhood, her mother having died giving birth to her.

Chanel met Misia in 1917 at the dinner party of actress and Chanel client Cécile Sorel in Paris. They hit it off immediately. Misia, with her statuesque physique and enigmatic character, was drawn to Chanel, 11 years her junior, for her natural allure and great style; that night Chanel wore a striking red, fur-trimmed velvet coat which caught Misia's eye. They met again the next day, at Chanel's atelier, and cemented a friendship that would last their lifetimes.

Triumph over hardship, and a passion for art and culture, bound them in what became an intense, sometimes strained, relationship. 'Misia has been my only woman friend,' Chanel would reveal, decades later. 'Misia gave me ample and countless reasons for liking her ... She is simultaneously the goddess of destruction and of creation.'

Through her love of the arts, Misia helped Chanel develop her interests, inspiration and style as well as a love for all things Russian; this influence would permeate her collections for years to come. Here, on the beach in the late 1920s, they are the picture of avant-garde sophistication.

To Venice,
in heartbreak

In 1919, Boy Capel died suddenly in a car crash, apparently on his way to see Chanel. Grief-stricken, she fled to Venice with Misia and her husband, the Spanish painter José Maria Sert in 1920. The dazzling Italian city gave Chanel time away to mourn and reflect, but also fuelled her with inspiration to take her forward.

In Venice, José Maria gave Chanel a tour of the city, enriching her artistic knowledge with visits to Baroque churches, Byzantine museums and numerous art galleries. 'With the Serts, Chanel managed not only to contain her enduring grief for the loss of Boy, but also to learn a huge amount from their cultural excursions,' says Isabelle Fiemeyer, in her book *Intimate Chanel*. 'As they wandered along the canals, Chanel was delighted to discover the symbol she held so dear, the emblematic lion that is everywhere in Venice, in stone, marble and bronze.'

Chanel was captivated by the magic of Venice – the architecture, the art, the Byzantine splendour, the Murano glass, the masked balls – and her time here inspired her greatly. She embodied the spirit of the city, and her style in Venice, whether she wore beach pyjamas or white linen suits, reflected a sophisticated new bohemian elegance that was to inspire a generation.

Patron of the arts

Through her friendship with Misia Sert, Chanel became a central figure in the avant-garde art scene. Sert was a great patron of the arts as well as a muse herself – she was painted by Henri de Toulouse-Lautrec, Pierre-Auguste Renoir and Pierre Bonnard. She was also friends with composers Claude Debussy and Maurice Ravel, writer Jean Cocteau and artist Pablo Picasso. This opened up a world of art, culture and endless inspiration for Chanel, which not only had a direct impact on her designs but also influenced how the artists dressed (Picasso rocked the Breton T-shirt throughout his life).

In 1922, playwright–poet Jean Cocteau asked Chanel to design the costumes for his play *Antigone* and around the time she was establishing her jewellery atelier, she also designed the costumes for *Le Train Bleu*, performed by the Europe-based touring company, the Ballets Russes. She became good friends with the dancers, including Serge Lifar, who famously lifted Chanel in a posed photograph, dressed in her signature masculine chic, in Venice, 1937.

Chanel was more than just an admirer of the great artists she hung out with; she also became a friend, supporter and confidante, especially to founder of the Ballets Russes, Sergei Diaghilev, and to fellow Russian emigré, composer Igor Stravinsky, to whom she gave a temporary home at her villa on the outskirts of Paris.

From Russia, with love

After a tough childhood, the death of Boy, and her two sisters (who she was still close to despite establishing herself in Paris) – all before 1920 – Chanel found herself alone, but not without direction. When times were tough, Chanel had a knack for making the best of it: enter Grand Duke Dmitri Pavlovich, who was reacquainted with Chanel in Biarritz in 1920 after meeting her in 1911. 'We dined together,' Chanel later told Paul Morand. 'I saw him the following day. In a very friendly way, I said to him: "I have just bought a little blue Rolls, let's go to Monte Carlo."'

Dmitri was the first cousin of Tsar Nicholas II and had been embroiled in the assassination of Rasputin, the Tsar's 'mystical adviser', in 1916, after which he had fled Russia in a bid to save his life. Chanel, feeling lonely and isolated, was completely captivated by the Slavic charm of Russia, and found Dmitri intriguing and irresistible. Dmitri, penniless and forlorn, found direction, glamour and emotional support from Chanel. 'It would have been impossible to find a better friend for that moment in time than dearest Coco,' Dmitri wrote in his diary.

'Coco devoted herself, in a way, to the pursuit of grandeur. She met the Duke of Westminster and, before him, Grand Duke Dmitri, with his extraordinary story. It was Dmitri who introduced her to the chemist Ernest Beaux,' said her great-niece Gabrielle Palasse-Labrunie in the book *Intimate Chanel*. This meeting with Beaux would lead to Chanel making her fortune by creating the best-selling scent of all time.

The power of pearls

Chanel adored jewellery and loved mixing precious stones with non-precious costume styles. She wasn't interested in expensive gemstones, but rather statement pieces that stood out. Pearls were ubiquitous, with most well-off women owning several strands. For Chanel, they were also a symbol of good luck, and they subtly illuminated the face, giving her famous black outfits a pop of contrast.

Pearls were not new – everyone, from Cleopatra to Queen Elizabeth I, had worn them – but Chanel gave them renewed allure. She wore multiple strands of different lengths for all looks, whether smart or casual, layering them with other pieces. She also popularised the simple pearl stud earring – Lydia Sokolova, principal dancer for Sergei Diaghilev's Ballets Russes, wore them while performing *Le Train Bleu* in 1924.

By that year, Chanel's busy costume jewellery workshop was creating statement, modern pieces, including oversized faux pearls which everyone, especially Americans, went mad about. New York department store Saks Fifth Avenue stocked bold shades of Chanel's fake pearls in blues, whites and reds. They were a sell-out success and furthered her reputation as the leading designer of the time.

'SOME
THINK L
THE OPP
POV
IT IS N
THE OPP
VULG

'SOME PEOPLE
THINK LUXURY IS
THE OPPOSITE OF
POVERTY.
IT IS NOT. IT IS
THE OPPOSITE OF
VULGARITY.'

— COCO CHANEL

'It was what I was waiting for.
A perfume like nothing else.
A woman's perfume, with the scent of a woman.'
– Coco Chanel

Making scents

In 1921, at the dawn of the Roaring Twenties, Chanel decided to shake things up in the fragrance world and launched a scent. Impeccably timed as ever, her first perfume encapsulated the modern spirit synonymous with her name by mixing natural ingredients with sophisticated new synthetic ones.

Chanel had recently met Russian-born perfumer Ernest Beaux, a soldier and chemist. Beaux experimented with chemical compounds (aldehydes) and Chanel, ever the trailblazer, loved the idea of these innovative substances and enlisted Beaux in the production of a new scent. 'It was what I was waiting for. A perfume like nothing else. A woman's perfume, with the scent of a woman,' Chanel said in later years.

When Beaux came back with various samples, she favoured number five – her lucky number and a rich, velvety mix that smelled like nothing you could name but which somehow reeked of modern luxury. Taking inspiration from the crisp, clean air of the Arctic Circle, Beaux had cleverly blended dozens of scents, including ylang-ylang, neroli, rose, sandalwood and jasmine from Grasse, into an instant best-seller.

The elegant glass bottle, apparently inspired by the angular symmetry of the Place Vendôme in Paris, with its simple rectangular stopper and timeless black-and-white label, became as iconic as the fragrance it held. To this day, over a century later, Chanel Nº5 remains one of the world's most popular scents.

An English affair

It was in Monte Carlo, in 1923, that Chanel met another of her most important love conquests, The Duke of Westminster, Hugh Richard Arthur Grosvenor, known as Bendor. He was over 6 feet tall, well built, rugged, and also the richest man in Britain, owning much of Mayfair and Belgravia in London, having inherited the Grosvenor family fortune. The affair, which lasted from early 1924 until 1930, was hugely important for them both.

Chanel soon became chatelaine of the duke's ancestral home in Cheshire, England. She was a great hostess. By now a formidable rider, she adored nature – which was handy as the duke's Reay Forest Estate, in the west of Scotland, covered almost 100,000 acres. 'Beneath his clumsy exterior, he's a skilful hunter. You'd have to be skilful to hang on to me for ten years. These ten years were spent very lovingly and very amicably with him,' she told Paul Morand in 1946. 'Westminster liked me because I was French. English women are possessive and cold. Men get bored of them.'

During the late 1920s, Chanel became absorbed by British style, thanks to the duke and it would dominate her aesthetic for the next few years. Everything, from the use of navy blue, which she observed on his yacht, *Flying Cloud*, to the style and practicality of tweed, which she adopted from the duke's shooting jackets, became hugely significant in her designs. The cardigan jacket, worn with a low-slung belt, that she wears here exemplifies the spirit of utility.

*'One is never over-dressed or underdressed
with a Little Black Dress.'*
– Karl Lagerfeld

The LBD is born

In 1926, with the jazz age in full swing, American *Vogue* published an illustration of a simple crêpe-de-chine black sheath dress, fitted to the knee, with slim sleeves, adorned with a simple string of pearls. As the epitome of simplicity, *Vogue* predicted that the Little Black Dress (LBD) would have mass appeal, comparing it to the popularity of the Ford automobile – 'Here is a Ford, signed Chanel' – and describing it as 'The frock that all the world will wear.'

Chanel, who had designed her first collection of LBDs in 1910, knew the impact it could have. With its simple, suits-all shape, the LBD became a huge success and, to this day, is a regular classic in every designer's repertoire – a byword for effortless glamour.

Designers in the following decades all paid homage to Chanel's LBD, from Hubert de Givenchy's iconic style for Audrey Hepburn in the 1961 film *Breakfast at Tiffany's* to Christina Stambolian's famous post-divorce 'revenge' dress for Princess Diana in 1994. Lagerfeld reinvented it in numerous guises each season, and any style icon worth her reputation has delivered a killer LBD look, knowing its power and eternal appeal.

But it is Gabrielle Chanel, the original purveyor of the look, who still epitomises its easy elegance. She wore a LBD throughout her life, with strings of illuminating pearls and a steely smile. Perfection.

Queen of Tweed

Tweed was a revelation for Chanel. The Duke of Westminster had several suits of tweed, mainly worn for shooting, and Chanel observed its durable yet comfortable qualities, adopting it for her own wardrobe and then for women everywhere.

She worked with the William Linton Mill in Cumbria, in the north of England, and reinvented the traditional Scottish fabric as a luxurious woven cloth for women's couture. She added lighter yarns, pastel shades and bolder hues, and her first tweed blazers, long in length and appealingly loose in silhouette, appeared in her Russian collections of the early 1920s. Tweed thereafter become a Chanel staple.

In the decades since Chanel turned tweed into a high-fashion fabric, it has remained in style, peaking in the 1960s when the world's most stylish women, from Jackie Kennedy to Elizabeth Taylor, wore it. Karl Lagerfeld cleverly renewed its appeal in the 1990s, with bold new hues including royal blue and canary yellow modelled on the catwalk by icons such as Linda Evangelista.

As with so many of her designs, it was Chanel who always wore it best – here, she wears an elegant tweed suit with a beret, pearls and waist-cinching belt. *Très chic*!

English traditions

Boy Capel had introduced Chanel to the etiquette and nuances of English society, but it was the Duke of Westminster who fully integrated her into British high society, introducing her to aristocrats and politicians, including future Prime Minister Winston Churchill, then Chancellor of the Exchequer. Who was impressed by both her physical and emotional strength.

On 27 January 1927, Churchill wrote to his wife Clementine: 'The famous Coco turned up and I took a great fancy to her – a most capable and agreeable woman – much the strongest personality Benny [Bendor, Duke of Westminster] has been up against. She hunted vigorously all day, motored to Paris after dinner and is today engaged in passing and improving dresses on endless streams of mannequins.'

Chanel, ever the graceful, unfazed social butterfly, happily hunted with Churchill and his son Randolph in 1928, wearing hunting attire done her way – a belted wool coat, sturdy leather boots and a practical riding hat – while still managing to look the epitome of chic. In his letter to Clementine, Churchill went on: 'She fishes from morning to night and has killed fifty salmon. She is very agreeable, really a great and strong being, fit to rule any man and an empire. Benny is … I think … extremely happy to be mated with an equal.'

4

The Boundary-Breaker

A designer with her models

By the early 1930s, despite having a workforce of over 2,400, Chanel remained hands-on in her atelier, wearing her scissors around her neck on a silk ribbon. Though she didn't make sketches, she told her studio head exactly what she had in mind and the model (or mannequin, as they were known) would be adorned before Chanel. The designer would take her scissors and adjust, snip and pin until she was happy, a process that could sometimes take an entire day.

'Nothing else existed for her, even the most important visitors had to wait,' explained her great-niece Gabrielle in *Intimate Chanel*, who would watch her in action in the rue Cambon salon. 'She would cut and cut again, cutting a suit or gown literally to shreds. Sometimes it was too awful to see those suits cut to pieces. She would pin and unpin, regularly pricking the mannequin, who would squeal in pain. She didn't speak either, as her mouth was full of pins.'

Chanel adored her models and had an almost maternal relationship with them, sitting with them calmly and giving them pep talks before presentations. She formed strong bonds over the decades with her favourites, including Marie-Hélène Arnaud, Suzy Parker and Odile de Croÿ. All of them remained loyal to Mademoiselle, as she was respectfully called, for the rest of her life.

Hollywood beckons

In the late 1920s, when studio mogul Samuel Goldwyn invited Chanel to go to Hollywood, attempting to lure her with a $1 million offer, she initially refused. She wasn't really a film fan and was unimpressed by the hype that surrounded Los Angeles but, after the Wall Street Crash in 1929, and with business down, she finally relented.

She arrived in March 1931, but things didn't go entirely smoothly. Chanel's most talked-about assignment in Hollywood was dressing Gloria Swanson for *Tonight or Never*. Chanel had designed a floor-length black satin dress for Swanson, who played an opera diva. Unbeknown to Chanel, Swanson, who was having an affair with Irish playboy Michael Farmer, was several weeks pregnant. Swanson wrote in her memoirs that Chanel 'glared furiously at me when I had trouble squeezing into one of the gowns she had measured me for'.

'You have no right to fluctuate in the middle of fittings,' Chanel told Swanson. 'Take off the girdle and lose five pounds!' In the end, Chanel resorted to putting her in rubberised corsets to conceal the growing bump. Despite all the hype, the film was a flop. Chanel had greater success with *The Greeks Had a Word for Them* featuring actress-of-the-moment Ina Claire. Both the film and the outfits were a hit and *Vanity Fair* nominated her to its 1931 Hall of Fame, 'Because she came to America to make a laudable attempt to introduce chic to Hollywood.'

Eternal elegance

'Elegance does not consist of putting on a new dress.'
– Coco Chanel

While other designers of the early 20th century, from Jean Patou to Elsa Schiaparelli, designed clothes very much of their era, Gabrielle Chanel created outfits that defied time. With her revolutionary looser silhouettes and modern fabrics, she was one of the first designers to create clothes with timeless appeal: a 1920s Chanel Little Black Dress, 1930s chiffon frock or 1960s tweed suit all still look as modern today as they did the first time they appeared in *Vogue*.

Chanel's secret? To focus on style and grace rather than fashion. 'Women are always too dressed up, but never elegant enough,' she told *Jours de France* in December 1961. The designer became obsessed with the concept of elegance to the extent that, in 1933, she contributed to the definition of 'French elegance as a component of dandyism' for the dictionary of the Société Baudelaire.

Chanel herself always set the best example, in terms of elegance, over the decades. Whether wearing a loose-cut cardigan suit with her signature strings of pearls, reclining in an LBD in her rue Cambon apartment or sitting at the dressing table of her suite at The Ritz in silk pyjamas, Chanel was always the epitome of timeless chic.

Red alert

Despite Chanel's much-documented obsession with monochrome,
the designer loved bold colours – especially red, which infiltrated her
collections more and more during the 1930s. 'In the street, people
stand back for a well-groomed woman in a bright colour (that suits
her), they let her go first, they admire her. Red is the colour of life and
blood, I love red,' she declared to *Elle* magazine in August 1963.

Her favourite hue was a deep, blood red, evident everywhere from the
red lacquered screens and leather-bound books of her rue Cambon
apartment to her favourite lipstick and the indulgent grosgrain
interior of her 2.55 bag. Even today, the Chanel makeup range has
dozens of killer red lipsticks, including Gabrielle, shade 444, in homage
to the designer.

Karl Lagerfeld revived red throughout his tenure at the label, making
it one of the Chanel colours of the 1980s – Princess Diana certainly
approved wearing a striking red coat and matching hat from the
1988/89 Chanel ready-to-wear collection on a trip to Paris in 1988.
Virginie Viard, creative director following Lagerfeld's death, also made
reference to Gabrielle's favourite shade with 1980s-inspired bold red
trenches, boxy jackets and pointy-toed shoes in her first solo collection
for the house in May 2019. *Vive le rouge*!

Woman in white

Chanel may be most famous for black, but she loved white in equal measure, understanding its head-turning impact. Although never known for creating bridal gowns, she did design white gowns for any occasion. 'I have said that black had everything. White too. They have an absolute beauty. It is perfect harmony. Dress women in white or black at a ball: they are the only ones you see,' she once said.

If the Little Black Dress was the hit of the 1920s, the elegant white bias-cut dress was the style of the more demure, post-Wall Street Crash world of the early 1930s. The white dress, in all its light and airy innocence, felt just right in the depths of the Depression, quite literally lightening the mood.

Chanel's white sailor-style flares had also become popular by this point, and much copied across the globe. White, too, was the colour of Chanel's hugely popular fake pearls, which dominated both the 1920s and 1930s.

White continued to be enormously important to Chanel, and she famously slept in white linen sheets wearing white silk pyjamas. In fact, Chanel wore white for every occasion, even Sergei Diaghilev's funeral, where both she and Misia Sert wore elegant white dresses, knowing the impresario loved seeing them in illuminating white.

'I DOI
FASH

I A
FASH

'T DO
ON.

M
ON.'

— COCO CHANEL

The Ritz

In 1935, Chanel left her apartment in the rue du Faubourg Saint-Honoré and moved into a suite at The Ritz, overlooking the Place Vendôme. It would be her home, on and off, for the next 36 years. Chanel was at the peak of her career, and having her every need catered for at The Ritz meant she had more time to focus on work.

Chanel felt right at home in the understated refinement of The Ritz, decorating her third-floor suite with her favourite furniture, including gilded mirrors, crystal chandeliers, art, lacquered screens and a velvet banquette. François Kollar captured a photo of Chanel in her suite, looking resplendent in a full-length black gown with elegant chiffon sleeves worn with her signature pearls and decorative flowers in her hair, next to a gilded mirror. Published in 1937, the picture illustrated the Chanel N°5 perfume advertisement.

During World War II, she continued to live at the hotel moving to a much smaller room at the back of the building. Although living elsewhere in the years after the war, Chanel returned for her 1950s comeback and stayed until her death in 1971. To this day, an Art Deco-inspired suite is named in her honour.

Bijoux de Diamants

'I wanted to cover women in constellations,' said Chanel in 1932, when she launched her boundary-breaking jewellery collection, Bijoux de Diamants. Applying couture principles to jewellery, her theme was a meteor shower of celestial diamonds plucked from the Parisian sky. With gemstones on loan from the Diamond Corporation in London, Chanel had reimagined diamonds, making them more wearable than the traditional pendant or choker styles that had come before, draping them over the skin in star formations and comets that looped around the neck. Many of them didn't even have clasps.

Chanel's high jewellery collection caused an outcry among the established male diamond merchants of Place Vendôme, who were threatened by a female dressmaker turning her hand to jewellery. So outraged were they that, after the short exhibition of the jewels, they demanded they were broken up and the diamonds returned. Happily, some of Chanel's designs sold and stayed intact.

Chanel had loved jewellery since the beginning of her career but ironically wasn't impressed by expensive gemstones. 'It's not the carats that count but the illusion,' she famously said. 'Jewels shouldn't make you look rich, they should make you look adorned.' Her artful use of pearls – layered up, oversized and mixed with precious and semi-precious stones – and bold, plastic costume jewellery, made by Maison Gripoix, meant that they became bestsellers, but it was her 1932 diamond collection that set the tone for the luxury Chanel jewellery range that still exists today.

'The camellia, with its minimalist lines, well-defined voluptuous
curves, and almost Art Nouveau designs, was destined to appeal
to her aesthetic and as an avant-garde designer.'
– Danièle Bott

The camellia

The simple, white flower had been making appearances both on her outfits and in her designs since the 1910s, whether clipped onto blouses, chiffon frocks or belts. In her book, *Chanel Collections and Creations*, Danièle Bott states: 'The camellia, with its minimalist lines, well-defined voluptuous curves, and almost Art Nouveau designs, was destined to appeal to her aesthetic and as an avant-garde designer.'

The camellia featured throughout the decades, whether on model Marie-Hélène Arnaud in *Marie Claire*, in September 1959, or Suzy Parker, shot by David Bailey with a simple white camellia in her hair in the early 1960s. In 1937, Chanel was photographed with her friend the artist Salvador Dalí, wearing one of her classic tweed suits with a pretty white camellia on the lapel, as ever donning the look she had created with supreme elegance.

Over the course of more than a century, the House of Chanel has fashioned the camellia in ceramic, silk, organza, feathers, leather and diamonds. It remains one of the company's most enduring emblems, appearing on everything from the handbag collection to jewellery and watches. Karl Lagerfeld created an entire wedding dress from camellias for the closing of the Chanel Couture show, in Autumn 2005, on Brazilian model Solange Wilvert. Pretty cool.

Chanel in colour

Gabrielle Chanel had become famous for her love of pared-back looks but, as the 1930s got going, she presented several uncharacteristically vibrant collections. The austere post-Wall Street Crash 1930s warranted some cheeriness, after all. Ever part of the zeitgeist, Chanel swapped her sober palette for colour, pattern and vibrancy, revelling in femininity and romanticism throughout the mid to late 1930s.

La Pausa, her Côte d'Azur villa, and its lush garden full of lavender, olive trees and climbing roses, as well as the natural land- and seascape around it, proved a huge inspiration during this period. In 1935, *Vogue* described her Blue collection as 'a mist of baby-blue tulle ... foaming towards the floor with a Pierrot ruche for a cape.'

Just a couple of years later, she presented a collection featuring shimmering gold lamé and silver sequins and, throughout this whole era, to cater for high society women going to frequent Parisian balls, experimented with lavish fabrics including silks, velvet and lace, albeit with a super-chic Chanel twist.

Her final foray into colour and pattern in that decade was her wonderfully extravagant Gypsy collection of 1939. On the brink of World War II, Chanel indulged in a romantic, more flamboyant mood, with an explosion of embroidered, coloured and exuberant full skirts. A final flourish to end an era.

Signs and symbols

'If you're born without wings, don't do anything to stop them growing,' said the famously aspirant Chanel. The feather, one of her favourite symbols, along with the ribbon and the camellia, signified her own free spirit.

Although famously no-nonsense, Chanel was also hugely superstitious, especially when it came to numbers. Her lucky number was 5: she always presented her collections on 5 February and 5 August; it was the number of her most famous scent, Chanel N°5; and she named her most celebrated bag – the 2.55 – after the date on which it was launched, February 1955.

Other symbols proved vital to Chanel's style iconography, from the lion (her star sign) that she discovered in abundance in Venice, which became an emblem on buttons (and ultimately featured five times on her grave) to the Maltese cross that harked back to her childhood in Aubazine. And let's not forget the iconic double-C logo, reminiscent of the abbey's stained-glass windows, as impactful today as it was a century ago.

5

A Pioneering Spirit

CHANEL SHUTS UP SHOP AS WORLD WAR II BREAKS OUT

Closure of the couture house

In 1939, with World War II looming, Chanel closed the doors of her couture house. She kept only the fragrance and accessories store at 31 rue Cambon open, partly in a bid to prevent the building becoming occupied by the Nazis. 'This is no time for fashion,' she declared. 'It is no longer the time to make dresses or to dress women whose husbands are going to be killed.'

The next few years proved challenging and, at times, controversial for Chanel thanks to her relationship with German officer Baron Hans Günther von Dincklage – who was part of the Nazi occupying force in Paris. She soon withdrew from the limelight and went into semi-retirement, spending the next few years between her suite at the Ritz, La Pausa, Switzerland and America.

Despite the war, Chanel's style was as sharp as it always had been. The designer – then in her 50s – remained as chic as ever, whether on the slopes of St Moritz, at the spas of Lausanne or in the garden of La Pausa.

Chanel later justified her closure of the couture house: 'I stopped working because of the war. Everyone in my place had someone who was in uniform – a husband, a brother, a father. The House of Chanel was empty two hours after war was declared.' It would be 15 years before Chanel returned to it.

A German affair

Chanel's lover during World War II was the towering, high-society
dandy Hans Günther von Dincklage, known as Spatz ('sparrow' in
German), who was 13 years her junior. Von Dincklage worked as an
attaché to the German ambassador and as a secret agent for the
Abwehr, the German military intelligence service.

Chanel's relationship with von Dincklage – who stayed with her at
The Ritz as well as at her rue Cambon apartment – could not help but
be controversial. Through von Dincklage, Chanel was able to travel
to both Madrid and Berlin to engage in covert operations with the
Germans in an effort to free her nephew, André Palasse, who had been
captured by the Germans.

According to some accounts, Chanel was unknowingly enrolled into
the Abwehr as a consequence. But a German espionage supervisor
revealed he had '... liberated her nephew, a war prisoner, the manager
of a silk factory in Lyon. Chanel never provided any intelligence.
I registered her as an agent to justify this intervention.'

Chanel later relied on the help of her old acquaintance Winston
Churchill to get her out of an awkward spot. Her great-niece, Gabrielle,
who lived with Chanel after the war, remembers her being arrested,
then returning home and saying, 'Churchill had me freed!'

The staircase
of dreams

There are few staircases in the world of fashion as iconic and instantly recognisable as the winding, mirrored staircase in Chanel's 31 rue Cambon couture house. Leading from the first floor to her legendary apartment stuffed with treasures and heirlooms, it was the backdrop to many of Mademoiselle's grandest moments.

'On the beige staircase, backed by great, slender faceted mirrors, overlooking the mannequins below, one might fall up or down the stairs any afternoon over an assortment of celebrities,' noted Sylvia Lan, for *Vogue*, in April 1929. Chanel's most memorable portraits were taken on that spot by the likes of Frank Horvat, Cecil Beaton and Robert Doisneau.

Chanel's rue Cambon staircase is still used in photo shoots, presentations and special events to this day. A memorable, more recent, snap is of former Spice Girl turned fashion designer Victoria Beckham photographed there with Karl Lagerfeld for French *Elle* in 2012.

The artist's muse

Chanel knew the power of art. And she lived through a transformative time in the European art scene, witnessing major art movements from Cubism to Art Deco via Surrealism. Chanel immersed herself in the Paris art scene thanks to introductions made by her great friend Misia Sert.

In 1926, as his Cubist phase ended, Dalí moved from Madrid to Paris and became part of the Surrealist movement. Around this time, he met Chanel. Like so many before him, Dalí fell for Chanel's charm. 'Chanel's originality was the opposite of mine,' Dalí later declared. 'I have always shamelessly exhibited my thoughts, while she neither conceals hers nor shows them off, but instead dresses them up ... She has the best-dressed body and soul on Earth.' In 1938, Dalí moved to La Pausa briefly and produced his complex, surreal masterpiece *Endless Enigma*.

Chanel hosted many decadent parties and gatherings over the years at which her artistic friends were fundamental. Here, surrounded by Jean Cocteau and Salvador Dalí, Chanel poses in her suite at the Ritz Paris for the January 1940 issue of American *Vogue*. The worlds of fashion and art have never collided quite so elegantly.

'YOU
GORGE
THIRTY, G
AT FOR
IRRESIST
THE R
YOUR

AN BE
OUS AT
HARMING
Y, AND
BLE FOR
ST OF
LIFE.'

— COCO CHANEL

The sportswoman

Chanel's childhood in rural France gave the designer a deep-rooted love of the countryside, fresh air and exercise. Chanel knew that clothes alone would not make a woman beautiful – it was all about having a healthy body and soul.

'The figure is more important than the face, and more important than the figure is the means by which you keep it. More important than all three is the enjoyment of life on your own basis, which is secured through good health,' she told journalist Djuna Barnes in 1931 in an article called 'Nothing Amuses Coco Chanel After Midnight.' 'Find out what it is that you like to do, and do it.' Chanel believed that posture, gestures and how a woman walked were key to her attractiveness.

'Work, then play, relax, swim, fish, do a turn at golf or tennis, get out in the open, enjoy the air and the sun ... if you want to have and to keep a charming figure and a flexible carriage, you must delight in the outdoors, fresh air, sports,' Chanel told Barnes. The designer practised what she peached and maintained her slim figure by not eating too much, by exercising and regularly visiting spas.

Chanel may have liberated women from the corset but she believed a healthy, toned physique was the basis for looking good. 'Yes, she had invented the shift dress, but she always thought women should make an effort,' says her biographer, Lisa Chaney.

The Swiss years

In 1945, Chanel escaped the gloom of Paris at the end of the war, and the difficult questions surrounding her relationship with von Dincklage, and went to Switzerland, to upper Lausanne on the bank of Lake Geneva. She was never idle, even though she wasn't working as a designer, and in that time created three perfumes under the name Mademoiselle Chanel: Nos 1, 2 and 31. She also indulged in beauty treatments at the Valmont Clinic and enjoyed visiting the Steffen tearoom in upper Montreux.

In 1947, Chanel signed a new contract with the Wertheimers (the family-owned business that financed, produced and distributed Chanel perfumes) whereby she would earn 2 per cent on all Chanel perfumes, as well as having her living expenses covered. Time spent in Switzerland was peaceful time for Chanel – it is no wonder she chose to be buried in Lausanne, her grave adorned by five stone lions, combining her lucky number with her favourite symbol.

Family values

Though Chanel barely knew her parents, she was deeply loyal to
her remaining family members. Of the five children, Chanel stayed
especially close to her sister Julia-Berthe and brother Alphonse before
the former's early and sudden death in 1912.

Chanel was also close to her father's younger sister, her aunt Adrienne,
because they were so close in age. As they had both worked as
seamstresses in Moulins after their schooling was finished, Chanel
roped Adrienne into helping when she launched her brand and the
subsequent shops.

Though she had no children of her own, when Julia-Berthe – a single
mother – died, Chanel took on the guardianship of her six-year-old
son André Palasse and raised him, sending him to a British boarding
school. The closeness of their bond was shown later, when he was
captured by the Germans in 1939 and she used her connections to
secure his release.

Chanel remained particularly close to André's daughter, her great-
niece Gabrielle Palasse-Labrunie, whom she affectionately nicknamed
'Tiny'. Palasse-Labrunie has been a rich source of information
about family life through her close relationship with her beloved
'Aunty Coco'.

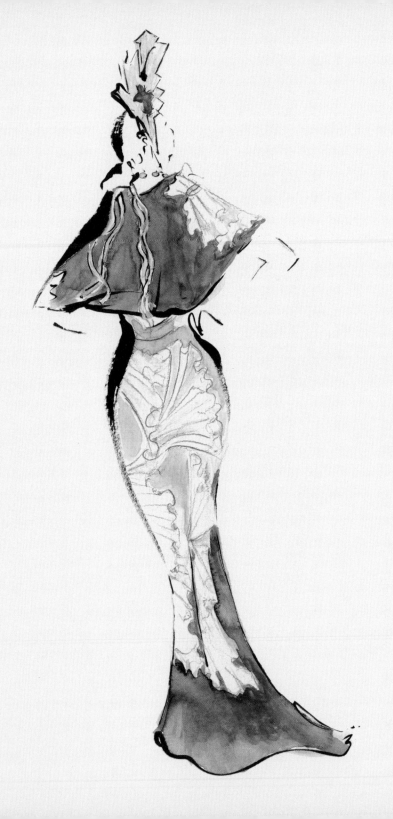

Chanel, the paradox

'I have a black being and a white being,' Chanel told Claude Delay. Though she may have hailed from humble beginnings and brought luxury to the masses though her perfume, Chanel was an unashamed elitist, admiring wealth and craving money and success. Like so many creative geniuses, Chanel was a woman of paradoxes.

Nowhere was this more evident than in her actual designs. Her styles for the 1920s may have appeared uncomplicated, but look closer and you will see fine craftsmanship that is anything but simple, as in the exquisite black shift dress she designed for American actress Ina Claire. Made from silk netting embroidered with sequins and featuring a silk lining, it's beautifully simple yet also incredibly intricate.

Despite being known for her masculine influences, Chanel was also ultra-feminine – her own appearance was the epitome of ladylike refinement. Having previously loosened the silhouette and encouraged women to stay slim and exercise, in the 1930s she unexpectedly indulged in colour and pattern, even briefly reviving the bustles and sculpted silhouettes she had so emphatically rejected in the 1910s and 1920s. She may not necessarily be remembered for this era, but it is just one element of the style paradox that was Coco Chanel.

The beauty of Chanel

'The face is a mirror that reflects the movements of your inner life: take great care of it,' Chanel told French *Vogue* in September, 1938.

Chanel's beauty and accessories shop on rue Cambon remained open throughout World War II, with demand surprisingly high. During wartime austerity, sales of *Vogue* magazine and makeup actually rocketed, as women craved a little glamour. In 1944, when Paris was liberated, American soldiers queued outside the rue Cambon shop to buy Chanel Nº5 for their wives and girlfriends back home.

Chanel had shown an uncanny knack for creating things people didn't even know they wanted when she debuted Chanel Nº5 in 1921. The following year, Ernest Beaux went on to create Chanel Nº22, named after the year in which it was created. Just two years after this, Chanel launched her first lip-colour collection – the rich formula was highly pigmented and arrived in luxurious ivory-coloured lipstick tubes with a natty copper sliding mechanism. Chanel's modern formula, Rouge Allure Intense Long-Wear Lip Colour, continues to be one of the best-selling lipsticks ever. The desirability of Chanel makeup and scents lives on – they remain as coveted today as they were over a century ago. Chanel succeeded in supplying the mass market without compromising the reputation of her luxury brand. It was no mean feat.

6

The Comeback Years

CHANEL RELAUNCHES HER LABEL AFTER THE WAR

Back with a bang

'I knew that one day, sooner or later, I'd resume my métier ... I was waiting for an opportune moment.'
– Coco Chanel

Almost ten years after the end of World War II, and in the midst of a glamour revival, much of which she deplored, Chanel, aged 71, was ready to make her comeback. In 1954, the Chanel salon on rue Cambon reopened with a cool, hard-hitting new collection that put a neat finger up to the overtly feminine fashion around at the time.

What had Chanel thought of Christian Dior's New Look of 1947 and the trend it had promoted? 'What a horror!' she exclaimed, on setting eyes upon the corseted bodices and full skirts. It gave Chanel the impetus to get back at the male designers who had dominated fashion since the end of the war, with their overly feminine silhouettes and old-fashioned ideas. With the financial backing of the Wertheimers, who still retained the perfume business, Chanel was able to relaunch her couture house.

'Her return to the Parisian scene represents far more than the reopening of a great maison de couture,' Jean Cocteau said in *Harper's Bazaar*, March 1954. 'She arrives as a sign that we must vanquish the inflation of mediocrity. Her instinct does not deceive her. The time has come when we must break with the fever of improvisation that troubles not only the surface of our city but its very depths.' Chanel was back.

Marilyn Monroe: a few drops of Chanel Nº5

In 1952, up-and-coming Hollywood siren Marilyn Monroe, then aged just 26, was fast becoming the most photographed woman in the world. With a few successful films under her tightly-cinched belt, including *The Asphalt Jungle* and *All About Eve*, the baby-faced blonde was in demand – everyone wanted to know everything about her. That year, she featured on the cover of *Life* magazine and, in the interview to accompany it, was asked what she wore to bed. She famously replied, 'Just a few drops of Chanel Nº5.'

Like Chanel, Monroe (born Norma Jeane Mortenson) had painfully humble beginnings – she never knew her father, and her mother ended up in an asylum. She subsequently had 12 sets of foster parents and also spent time in an orphanage. At the age of 16, she married factory worker James Dougherty to escape her ghastly childhood. Her marriage over, in 1946 she was signed by Twentieth Century Fox and became the blonde Hollywood icon.

Launched five years before Monroe was born, by 1952 Chanel Nº5 was already a hit across the globe, but Monroe's endorsement cemented its popularity for decades more. Chanel Nº5 subsequently became synonymous with a string of celebrities including actresses Catherine Deneuve, Ali McGraw and Nicole Kidman, who have all fronted its ad campaigns.

Chanel's new look

When Chanel launched her comeback collection in 1954, there was one model who was key to its success – red-headed American beauty Suzy Parker, who would become the inspiration for Audrey Hepburn's 1957 role in *Funny Face*. Wearing Chanel's first new outfit, a navy suit with a bow tie, she set the tone for the low-key, elegant presentation that Chanel was aiming for. She also secured American interest – a crucial market for Chanel's future success.

Suzy defined glamour in the 1950s and brought personality to the equation, setting the bar for the first generation of supermodels. Since World War II, models had started to become celebrities in their own right, and Chanel was quick to spot this opportunity. Although the French press were lukewarm about Chanel's comeback, now favouring her male competitors including Dior and Balenciaga, buyers were interested, and Parker was photographed with Chanel for an iconic cover of French *Elle* magazine.

Alongside her dazzling beauty (Dior called Suzy 'the most beautiful woman in the world'), Chanel adored Suzy's spark and she became something of a mentor. When Suzy gave birth to her first child in 1959, she named her Georgia Belle Florian Coco Chanel. Naturally, Chanel became her godmother.

Marie-Hélène Arnaud

When Chanel debuted her comeback collection on 5 February 1954, the well-connected French model Marie-Hélène Arnaud played a crucial role. Alongside the professional models, such as Suzy Parker, Chanel wanted real women ('with bosoms and hips – with a real shape – they must have elegance,' as she put it) to model in her show rather than nameless mannequins. So she asked Arnaud to bring in her high-profile friends, including Countess Mimi d'Arcangues, Claude de Leusse and Princess Odile de Croÿ.

Chanel cleverly allowed her new set (or *cabine*, as she referred to them) to keep the clothes they modelled, and thus they became brilliant ambassadors for the label. And the foundations were laid for models to be personalities. Here was a group of influencers, in the century before social media was even invented.

Bettina Ballard, editor of American *Vogue*, featured Arnaud in the March 1954 issue, with photos by Henry Clarke. She wore three outfits, including a red V-neck dress with pearls and a classic navy jersey suit with a padded-shouldered cardigan jacket and neat A-line skirt. In other words, it was the epitome of understated chic and a world away from the super-feminine housewifely looks Dior and his pals were dishing out. The looks Arnaud modelled were an instant hit with Americans and Chanel's comeback success was secured.

'YOU L

ON

YOU

AS

BE AM

VE BUT
CE;
AIGHT
VELL
SING.'

— COCO CHANEL

The first proper designer handbag is born

With the Chanel comeback in full swing, thanks to the massive commercial success of her new designs, particularly in the huge American market, the canny designer decided to launch the 2.55 bag in February 1955, with the name coming from the date of its launch. And if there's one bag to top all handbags in terms of desirability and status as an icon of design, it is Chanel's famous quilted, chain-handled 2.55 bag.

Fed up with carrying her handbag in her arms, Chanel had designed a pouch in the early 1920s inspired by the practicality of soldiers' satchels. In 1955, she added quilting and the famous gold chain, with a black leather cord and a rectangular clasp. With its deep red interior and useful pockets, the bag was not only liberating (no hands required) but also deeply luxurious.

Chanel kept just a jewelled cigarette box, a lipstick and a powder compact in her own 2.55, along with a little note that said, 'We are all dust, and the most important thing is that we dream'. 'Her dream of being independent and liberated is summed up in that bag,' said Amanda Harlech, Karl Lagerfeld's 'second pair of eyes' at Chanel from 1997 until his death in 2019.

Two-tone pumps step into style

In 1957, now three years into her killer comeback, Chanel decided to launch a new kind of shoe. Featuring beige uppers, a black-tipped toe and a comfortable 5 cm (2 in) heel that meant it was neither too tall nor too stubby, the press hailed them 'the new Cinderella shoe'. The design had the remarkable ability to flatter the foot and elongate the leg of anyone who slipped them on. Raymond Massaro, the Chanel chief shoemaker at the time, said, 'The black, slightly square toe shortened the foot.'

Perhaps inspired, in part, by the English gents Chanel had known – including Boy Capel and the Duke of Westminster, who both wore two-tone brogues – the style was an instant hit, and snapped up by stylish European actresses of the moment including Romy Schneider, Catherine Deneuve and Brigitte Bardot. 'You leave in the morning with beige and black, you dine with beige and black, you go for a cocktail with beige and black. You're dressed from morning to evening!' Chanel said, when presenting them for the first time. Karl Lagerfeld added the ballet-pump version in 1986, and this also remains a classic.

Mad about Liz

In the early 1960s, there was one American actress with whom everyone was obsessed: Elizabeth Taylor. In 1962, during the time she was filming *Cleopatra* and having an affair with co-star Richard Burton, Taylor arrived in Paris in top-to-toe pink Chanel. Liz oozed Hollywood glamour and garnered press attention like no other. This appearance heralded a new era for the Parisian brand.

Elizabeth Rosemond Taylor was born in London on 27 February 1932 to American parents, who later moved back across the Atlantic and settled in Los Angeles as war loomed in Europe. Her mother was a stage actress and her father an art dealer. In 1942, Taylor made her first film, *There's One Born Every Minute*, and by 1960 had won an Academy Award for her performance as a call girl in *Butterfield 8*. It was Taylor's extraordinary natural beauty – those striking violet-blue eyes, curtain-like dark lashes and a figure to die for – along with her charisma on screen that made her one of Hollywood's hottest names.

Along with Romy Schneider, Jeanne Moreau and Jane Fonda, Taylor gave Chanel the star quality that propelled the brand into a glamorous new era.

An unforgettable moment

There were many historic and memorable days in the 20th century, but few as agonisingly unforgettable as 22 November 1963. An ever-immaculate Jackie Kennedy walked from the plane in Dallas next to her husband, the President of the USA, John F. Kennedy, wearing a Chanel-designed bouclé tweed suit in bubblegum pink. The neat two-piece had been made in Paris and fitted in New York by Chez Ninon, and came with a quilted navy collar, neat square pockets and gold buttons. The look was finished with a matching pillbox hat and gloves.

As First Lady, she had established herself as one of the most stylish women in the world, with a heap of fashion admirers emulating her style. At 12.30 pm on that fateful day, while riding in a motorcade through Dealey Plaza in downtown Dallas, Texas, JFK was shot dead by a mystery assassin. 'Lady Bird' Johnson, wife of the Vice President, who had been riding in the car behind, later recalled how she saw 'a bundle of pink, just like a drift of blossoms, lying on the back seat. I think it was Mrs Kennedy, lying over the President's body.'

Jackie kept the blood-spattered suit on for the rest of the day and it became a powerful symbol of stoicism in the face of trauma and tragedy. She told aides who urged her to change on the plane back home, 'Let them see what they have done.'

Years later, she told reporters that her husband had said before the trip: 'There are going to be all these rich, Republican women at that lunch ... wearing mink coats and diamond bracelets. And you've got to look as marvellous as any of them. Be simple, show these Texans what good taste really is.' She achieved that and so much more.

The allure of Brigitte Bardot

The Parisian 'sex bomb' proved to be one of Chanel's sassiest – and most influential – fans. At the pinnacle of her career, in the late 1950s and early 1960s, Brigitte Bardot wore Chanel, giving it a modern new edge and securing its popularity among the hard-to-please French. The contrast worked: the clean, loose lines of Chanel accentuated her famous curves in the most subtle way.

Bardot, who had appeared on the cover of French *Elle* magazine as a 'junior model' at the tender age of 15, went on to become an actress and one of France's most paparazzied women, her coquettish beauty drawing audiences in their droves. In 1965 she even appeared as herself in the American-made *Dear Brigitte* with James Stewart, though, oddly, she was only in one scene. Just before she turned 40, Brigitte retired from the limelight to focus on animal rights activism, her role in securing Chanel's reputation as one of the chicest labels of the 1960s complete.

Chanel, a grand finale

'May my legend prosper and thrive. I wish it a long and happy life,' Chanel famously said towards the end of her life.

In her final years, with many friends and acquaintances dead, Chanel was lonely and, although proud of her immense success and achievements, said to her great-niece, Gabrielle, 'In the end it was you who was right, Tiny: you have a husband, children, a proper life, and I am alone.'

But when we look back at her immense achievements, there was no reason for her to have felt melancholy. Chanel had lived an utterly incredible life, full of love, passion, creativity, art and monumental success. She had changed the way women dressed forever, liberating them from restrictive corsets and overly frilly clothing, building a global fashion empire that has lasted well beyond her death.

Her last great achievement was launching the perfume Chanel No.19 on her birthday (19 August 1970), the year before her death. On 10 January 1971, aged 87 and less than a month from completing her Spring/Summer couture collection, Chanel complained to her maid Céline of abdominal pain. Dressed in a classic suit which she'd worn to work that day, she slipped beneath the crisp white sheets of her bed at the Ritz and drew her last breath. Her final words apparently: 'This is how one dies.'

Chanel's funeral service took place at the Church of the Madeleine, Paris, which was packed with Chanel employees, models and members of high society. Next to her grave in Lausanne, Switzerland, marked by the tombstone she had designed herself, she had asked for a bed of white flowers and a little bench so people could come and chat to her.

7

The Legend Lives On

KARL LAGERFELD DELIVERS CHANEL TO A NEW GENERATION

Kaiser Karl

In 1983, 12 years after Gabrielle Chanel's death, Hamburg-born Karl Lagerfeld took the reins at the iconic French brand as its first creative director. Lagerfeld had first been hired by Pierre Balmain in 1955, and had gone on to design for Chloé, Valentino and Fendi. He was the perfect man for the job. His USP? A fiercely forward-thinking approach, ability to draw inspiration from the street up, and a larger-than-life personality. Plus, that jaunty fashion ponytail!

Lagerfeld immersed himself in the Chanel archive, while also planning something radically new. He knew that, for Chanel to survive, he would need to reinvent the brand for a new customer: the fun, flash-your-cash 1980s generation. His debut couture show for Chanel for Spring/Summer 1983 saw him rework Chanel's classic suit, this time with sleek jackets nipped-in at the waist and accentuated at the shoulders, worn with swishy skirts and two-tone court shoes. These were all delivered with glossy bobs and strands of pearls. Here were clothes for the modern working woman.

Over subsequent collections, Lagerfeld – who had a reputation for his great wit and acerbic one-liners – took Chanel in ever bolder directions. He exaggerated classic Chanel icons, making the interlocking Cs, quilted bags, chain belts and pearls bigger and brasher. He injected bright, clashing colours never seen at Chanel before. He gave Chanel a radical new identity and pushed boundaries to keep the brand relevant with everyone from rappers to rich Parisians. No doubt Mademoiselle would have raised an eyebrow – and maybe a smile too.

The supers do Chanel

By the mid-1980s, there was a new troupe of women taking the world
by storm: the 'supermodels'. Linda Evangelista, Cindy Crawford, Naomi
Campbell and Helena Christensen led the way. This leggy catwalk
army dominated magazine covers and influenced a whole generation
of wannabes. Lagerfeld had enlisted 1980s icons Jerry Hall and Ines de
la Fressange as Chanel models from the beginning, and now he wanted
to add to his coterie. Like Gabrielle Chanel, Lagerfeld knew the power
of having the world's most glamorous women behind the brand.

In the early 1990s, Claudia Schiffer became one of Lagerfeld's
most important muses. Having seen her first British *Vogue* cover,
photographed by Herb Ritts for the October 1989 issue, Lagerfeld
was smitten. Mesmerised by her delicate blonde beauty, reminiscent
of a 1960s Brigitte Bardot, Lagerfeld knew Schiffer had the look to
propel the brand into the next decade and hired her for his next
Chanel campaign. He would often finish his shows with Schiffer
as the all-important Chanel bride. 'To [me as] his muse, he was my
mentor, a profoundly cultured, kind and charismatic man, with an
extraordinary mind and an unparalleled vision,' Schiffer told *Vogue*,
paying tribute to Lagerfeld in 2019.

Tweed remixed

When Chanel originally introduced the tweed suit in the early 1920s, in the form of a boxy jacket worn with a calf-length straight cut skirt, it was revolutionary. Over the decades, the tweed suit became the Chanel weathervane, changing with the times to fit new trends. Yet it always maintained a wearable simplicity. When Lagerfeld arrived at the house in 1983, he was quick to revive this Chanel classic but, this time, served up for the 1980s generation.

Welcome to his bold new interpretations of tweed! Jumbo weaves, gold threading and punchy colours, including fuchsia pinks, electric blues and ultraviolets, worn by icons including Naomi Campbell and Linda Evangelista. This was Chanel, but not as we knew it. Lagerfeld played with proportions, creating giant houndstooth tweed, and introduced bold colours including snappy bright red and pink.

One of his most radical reinventions of tweed was for Autumn/Winter 1991; Chanel favourite Evangelista wore a fuchsia-pink tweed zip-up jacket with a cornflower-blue pencil skirt and matching pink tweed beret. With her jumbo pearls, in hues of pink, and oversized chain belt, Evangelista was a picture of edgy early 1990s fun. Bam! Tweed was back in style for a bold new era.

Princess power

After becoming engaged to Prince Charles in February 1981, at the tender age of 20, Lady Diana Spencer became an overnight trendsetter. Everyone wanted a piece of her innocent charm – the bashful, fluttery eyed blonde who instantly captured the nation's hearts. Whether she wore a casual koala-print sweater, smart skirt suit or pie-crust collar and pearl earrings, a new generation of young women wanted to look exactly like Diana, hair flicks and all.

By the time Diana married Prince Charles in July 1981 at St Paul's Cathedral in London, wearing an ivory silk-taffeta gown with an extravagantly long train, by David and Elizabeth Emanual, she was a fully-fledged style icon. It was only natural that she would gravitate towards Chanel. In 1988, she made a striking statement by wearing a scarlet-red, calf-length Chanel coat on a trip to Paris. A bold choice for a Princess gaining in sartorial confidence. Perhaps her most polished Chanel outfit was the powder-blue bouclé suit with matching pillbox hat she wore for Prince William's confirmation in March 1997; a picture of poise and elegance just five months before her untimely death.

The power of celebrity

During his tenure at Chanel, Lagerfeld built relationships with key celebrities who would end up becoming all-important brand ambassadors, just as Gabrielle Chanel had done in the 1950s and 1960s.

In 1987, there was one French girl dominating the airwaves: the gamine 14-year-old Vanessa Paradis. 'Joe Le Taxi' was a huge hit in 15 countries – all of them mad for her cute French accent and gap-toothed gorgeousness. That one song helped launch her on a path that would lead to worldwide fame, a successful modelling career and a relationship with pin-up actor Johnny Depp (their daughter Lily-Rose Depp has been a Chanel ambassador since 2015).

Lagerfeld was quick to spot Paradis potential as a style icon and in 1991, when she was 19 years old, claimed her as one of his Chanel models. Paradis famously swung from a glamorous trapeze swing wearing black feathers in the advertisement for Coco, L'esprit de Chanel; she was perfect for the scent, which had been released in 1984 to appeal to a younger new customer. A new generation of Chanel fans was entranced.

The ultimate vamp

If there's one film that defined the look and vibe of the 1990s, it's Quentin Tarantino's cult 1994 picture *Pulp Fiction*. Starring John Travolta, Samuel L. Jackson and Uma Thurman – who played the troubled underworld moll Mia Wallace. Mia had a very distinctive look: a slick black bob, crisp white shirt and black–red nails in a new shade everyone wanted to know about: Chanel's Rouge Noir.

Rouge Noir (known as Vamp in the USA) was created by Chanel's director of makeup Heidi Morawetz. Morawetz made it at the last minute, backstage, for Chanel's Autumn/Winter 1994 catwalk show, by mixing red and black to create the distinctive reddish black we all recognise. Soon, nail polish was more fashionable than it had ever been. When it was launched in the USA, there were queues outside Barneys store in New York and a news piece on CNN. In the UK, it sold out within a day and had a 6–12 month waiting list. As a result, it achieved cult status and become the nail colour of the 1990s, making it Chanel's best-selling item of makeup ever.

Throughout the 1990s and 2000s, Morawetz worked alongside Dominique Moncourtois, Chanel's international director of makeup creation, and between them they made Chanel cosmetics as coveted as the fashion itself.

'YOU
THE C
THING
WORLD IN
AND JEA
UP TC

AN BE
ICEST
N THE
A T-SHIRT
IS – IT'S
YOU.'

— KARL LAGERFELD

Hip haute

In 1993, American photographer Steven Meisel was due to shoot a group of edgy young British women for a British *Vogue* story 'Anglo-Saxon Attitude'. *Vogue* assistant Plum Sykes brought friend-of-a-friend Stella Tennant – a 6-ft tall aristocrat with a pixie cut and ring through her septum – to the attention of stylist Isabella Blow. Blow, instantly loving Tennant's rebellious look, booked her for the job. Meisel was spellbound. Before she knew it, Tennant had been booked for a Versace campaign, was starring on the cover of Italian *Vogue* and had moved to New York to become a top model.

Granddaughter of the Duke and Duchess of Devonshire, Tennant had an irresistible aristo-punky vibe that defined the look of fashion in the late 1990s. Having trained in sculpture at Winchester College of Art, she had a refreshingly defiant attitude to fashion that made her a favourite with subversive designer Alexander McQueen. Suddenly, her nonchalant, androgynous look was in demand and Karl Lagerfeld, always part of the zeitgeist, made Tennant the face of Chanel in 1996, replacing Claudia Schiffer

Whether wearing a micro bikini, with just a double-C logo to cheekily conceal the nipples, or a classic monochrome suit, Tennant encapsulated the free, independent Chanel spirit. Chanel's creative director, Virginie Viard, paid homage to the late model after her untimely death in 2020, with Chanel's Autumn/Winter 2021 show. 'Today, some of these silhouettes make me think of Stella Tennant's allure; the way she wore certain pieces, it was so Chanel,' Viard said before the show. Tennant-inspired pieces included a monochrome tweed kilt with wool leggings and bold Fair Isle knits with Oxford bag trousers and flat shoes. It was Chanel, through and through.

Penélope Cruz

Spanish actress Penélope Cruz has been one of Chanel's most enduring fans. With numerous appearances on the red carpet wearing exquisite custom-made Chanel haute couture, Cruz encapsulates Gabrielle Chanel's original spirit of elegance and refinement. No wonder Lagerfeld, a long-time friend and admirer, made Cruz the face of the Chanel Cruise collection in 2018.

Cruz made her name in the 1992 film *Belle Époque*, which won an Oscar for best foreign film. She soon became muse to Spanish director Pedro Almodóvar, appearing in his 1997 film *Live Flesh* and, in 1999, *All About My Mother* and fast became a red-carpet favourite. From Cannes to Hollywood, Cruz has rocked Chanel with an elegance like no other, whether in floor-length red silk taffeta, frothy cream tulle or black organza.

Cruz wore an exquisite haute couture Chanel dress to the Academy Awards for her 2021 film Madres paralelas (Parallel Mothers). The head-turning dress took an impressive 680 hours of work, thanks to over 8,000 embroidered elements including a metallic-effect tweed necklace which acts as the halter-neck. Touchingly, Cruz walked in Lagerfeld's ski-chalet-inspired posthumous final show (Autumn/ Winter 2019) for the fashion house, at the Grand Palais Museum in Paris, wearing a fluffy white skirt, layers of ruffles and wedge boots – an emotional tribute to her friend and collaborator.

Mademoiselle Moss

It was only a matter of time before the Londoner and waifish wonder that is Kate Moss found her way onto the Chanel catwalk and fronted one of its highly coveted fragrance campaigns. Lagerfeld first spotted the then 19-year-old Moss on the cover of British *Vogue* for its March 1993 issue, wearing a bouclé tweed Chanel bustier and boasting a dewy, doe-eyed beauty that felt brand new. He declared, 'She's the free girl of our times.'

Moss heralded a cool new era for Chanel and became a fixture at its shows from that moment on. She took on an array of personas for the French fashion house, from a punky, pink-haired gamine for Spring/Summer 1994 to cool urban working girl for the Autumn/Winter 1997 collection. For the latter, she appeared on the catwalk wearing a chic, baggy brown tweed suit teamed with a micro-leather, camellia-encrusted bra.

In 2001, Moss became the face of the Coco Mademoiselle fragrance campaign, appearing as a host of different characters. But in 2004 Chanel famously ditched Moss when details of her party antics hit the tabloid-newspaper front pages, later replacing her as the face of Coco Mademoiselle with the actress Keira Knightley.

Beyoncé rocks Chanel

Lagerfeld loved pop culture – and it was a two-way relationship. By the late 1990s and early 2000s, a new generation of music artists were drawn to the brand. Enter Texas-born superstar Beyoncé to help give the label a healthy new dose of street cred. Beyoncé Giselle Knowles rose to fame in the late 1990s as the lead singer of the R&B band Destiny's Child, with Michelle Williams and Kelly Rowland.

Her first solo album, *Dangerously in Love*, was released in 2003 and went on to win five Grammys. By this time she had become one of the most adored pop stars of the whole decade, famous for her powerful voice, 'twerky' dance moves and the mother of all bodies. Whether in the form of oversized double-C logo earrings or bold new interpretations of the tweed jacket, layered with gold chains with gigantic Chanel logos, Beyoncé has always worn the brand with bold aplomb, making Chanel all her own.

The superstar set the tone, making the brand accessible to a new generation of 21st-century musicians including L'il Kim, Lily Allen, Rihanna, Pharrell Williams and Billie Eilish. More recently the brand has engaged with K-pop sensations G-Dragon and Jennie, taking Chanel to new arenas and keeping the brand alive and relevant.

Like a Virginie

Virginie Viard arrived at Chanel in 1987, just three years into Lagerfeld's tenure. Her natural talent shone through, and she fast rose through the ranks to become, as Karl put it, 'my right arm and my left arm'. In the last few seasons of Lagerfeld at Chanel, Viard joined him for the catwalk bow – there could have been no greater recognition of her importance.

Born in Lyon, France, to parents who were both doctors, Viard studied theatre design, but fashion was in the blood – she was taught to sew by her mother, and her grandparents were silk manufacturers. She started her career as an assistant to costume designer Dominique Borg before landing a job at Chanel. In 1992, Viard followed Lagerfeld to Chloé, before returning to Chanel to become studio director. A Chanel thoroughbred, Viard was the obvious choice to succeed Lagerfeld following his death.

Viard's first show for Chanel was Cruise 2020, held in the Grand Palais, Paris, just three months after Lagerfeld's death, and it was a lesson in modern refinement. Adhering to Gabrielle Chanel's core values, Viard's clothes are designed so that women feel comfortable and confident. Under Viard, Chanel once again has a woman designing easy, elegant and super-wearable pieces – softer and with less hype but totally right for the next era. She is a modern woman, Chanel to the core, designing clothes women want to wear. *C'est si bon!*

Bibliography

Bott, Danièle, *Chanel: Collections and Creations,*
Thames & Hudson Ltd, London, 2007

Chaney, Lisa, *An Intimate Life,* Penguin,
London, 2012

Charles-Roux, Edmonde, *Chanel and Her
World: Friends, Fashion, and Fame,* Vendome
Press, London, 2005

Cosgrave, Bronwyn, *Vogue on Coco Chanel,*
Quadrille Publishing Ltd, London, 2012

Dalí, Salvador, *The Secret Life of Salvador Dalí,*
Dover Publications, London, 1993

Delay, Claude, *Chanel Solitaire,* Gallimard,
Paris, 1983

Ewing, Elizabeth, *History of 20th Century
Fashion,* Batsford, London, 2005

Fiemeyer, Isabelle, *Intimate Chanel,*
Flammarion, Paris, 2011

Hess, Megan, *Coco Chanel: The Illustrated World
of a Fashion Icon,* Hardie Grant, London, 2015

Haedrich, Marcel, *Coco Chanel, Her Life, Her
Secrets,* Paris, 1979

Manchester, William, *The Death of a President:* November 1963, Harper & Row, New York, 1967

Morand, Paul, *The Allure of Chanel,* Hermann, London, 1976

O'Hara Callan, Georgina, *Dictionary of Fashion and Fashion Designers,* Thames & Hudson, London, 2008

Picardie, Justine, *Coco Chanel: The Legend and the Life, by Justine Picardie,* Harper Collins, London, 2017

Wilcox, Claire, *The Golden Age of Couture: Paris and London 1947–57,* V&A Publishing, London, 2008

Worsley, Harriet, *Decades of Fashion,* Konemann, London, 2006

Acknowledgements

The author would like to thank Cécile Goddet Dirles in the Chanel archive in Paris; Natalie Lukaitis, Harriet Davies and Laura Behaegel in the Chanel Patrimoine; illustrator Nicola Sutcliffe; art director Maeve Bargman; writers Dan Jones, Bronwyn Cosgrave, Alfred Tong and Justine Picardie; and Chelsea Edwards at Hardie Grant. Finally, her husband Tim Westhead for his support and excellent cooking.

About the Author

Maggie Davis is a style journalist and digital editor based in London. After studying at the London College of Fashion in the late '90s, she went on to work on the fashion desks at *Vogue*, *ES Magazine* and *Time Out*. She has since run a successful kids style blog and worked as a consultant for fashion brands.

About the Illustrator

After qualifying with a first-class degree in fashion design, Nicola Sutcliffe produced and sold her own label for 15 years. In recent years she has returned to her love of fashion illustration, exhibiting with the Fashion Illustration Gallery, and has been commissioned by clients including Vue Cinema and Poster Space.

Published in 2022 by Hardie Grant Books, an imprint of
Hardie Grant Publishing

Hardie Grant Books (London)
5th & 6th Floors
52–54 Southwark Street
London SE1 1UN

Hardie Grant Books (Melbourne)
Building 1, 658 Church Street
Richmond, Victoria 3121

hardiegrantbooks.com

British Library Cataloguing-in-
Publication Data. A catalogue record
for this book is available from the
British Library.

Chanel: Style Icon by Maggie Davis
ISBN: 9781784885670

Publishing Director: Kajal Mistry
Senior Editor: Chelsea Edwards
Design: Maeve Bargman
Copy Editor: Jessica Spencer
Proofreader: Gaynor Sermon

Colour Reproduction by p2d
Printed and bound in China
by Leo Paper Products Ltd